To my two precious grands and any future grands—
Grammy wrote this for you!

To God, You stretch me daily to be intentional about my legacy while modeling how to love lavishly.

You made me grand

by Meg Wilson | art by Marieke van der Vlies

New Wake Press

Published in 2021
by New Wake Press
www.YouMadeMeGrand.com

Copyright © 2019

All rights reserved. No part of this publication may be reproduced or transmitted in any form or by any means, electronic, or mechanical, including photocopying, recording, or by any information storage and retrieval system, without permission in writing from the publisher.

ISBN: 978-1-7369544-0-9

Written by Meg Wilson
Illustrated by Marieke van der Vlies

Our nest had been empty just a short while.
Left were sweet memories like your mom's toothless smile.

After raising our children, we watched as they flew.
A few weddings later, our gatherings grew.

We settled into a world, filled with grown-ups,
One big announcement would change that set up.
My baby was expecting a new baby at hand.
And I started dreaming about being Grand.

My new name was given a great deal of thought;
Would I be Grammy, Mimi, or not?
Some Grand-names are passed down without much ado.
But for me this grand role deserved something new.

Several of my friends already had grandkids.
I could always tell by their goofy ol' grins.
I wondered as they beamed, "What is the big deal?"
Still we counted the days, though it felt so unreal.

Every Grand wonders, will you be a boy or a girl?
Would your hair be stick-straight or naturally curl?
Excitement was brewing as your arrival drew near.
More anxious this time than for my little dears.

Then the day came - it was time - you were coming!
Your mother called, we cheered and came running.

After some hard work by your mom, you popped out.
We soaked in every detail; you were ours, with no doubt.

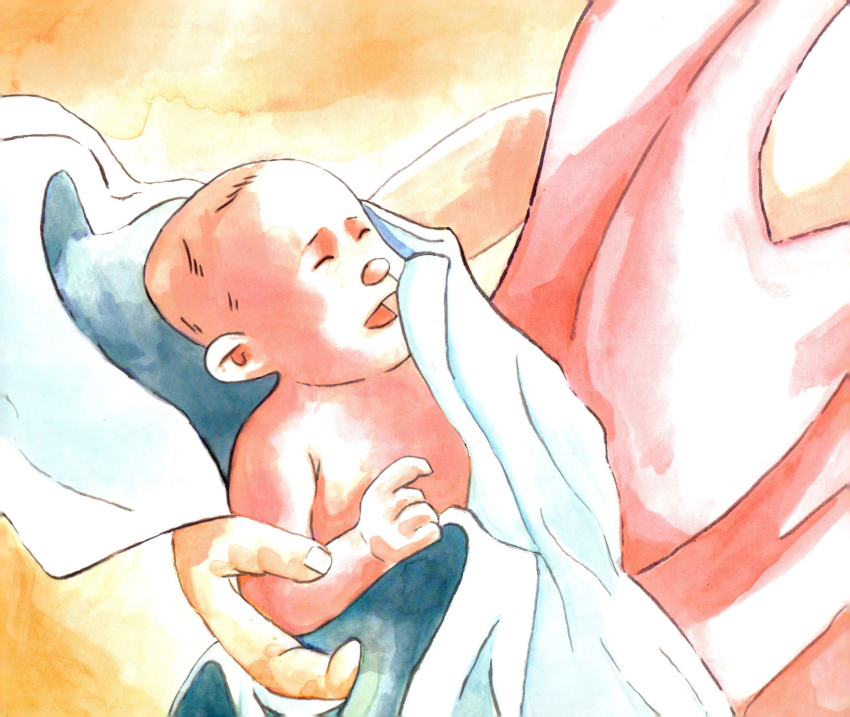

I reached ever so gently for your delicate hand.
And got the first hint of what it meant to be Grand.
When You held on, the unexpected took place,
Something amazing as I gazed on your face.

A door in my heart I didn't know existed,
Flung open with new feelings that couldn't be resisted.
Rainbows and butterflies released from within,
My face began shining with a goofy ol' grin.

I looked at my daughter, and back at your hand.
Everything's brighter since you made me Grand!

About the Author

Meg Wilson and her husband of 38 years have two grown daughters, and they are "Grands" to two (so far) precious children. She has always loved the written word and pursued various types of writing. Her first published work was the nonfiction book, *Hope After Betrayal* but, her love for children's books was still calling. Meg believes it is important to be intentional about legacy. After the birth of her first grandchild, all of the new feelings had to find a voice and *You Made Me Grand* was the result.

About the Illustrator

Raised with music, books and cartoons, Marieke van der Vlies was deeply in love with drawing and writing at an early age. She graduated at the art academy ArtEZ in Zwolle and finished her Bachelor studies in Illustration – Stories and Design. Stories are all around us, at work, on the street. It's why she prefers to be on-the-go, outdoors where she lives in the Netherlands. She often combines traditional methods with less traditional ways of working. As a result, her work is best characterized by versatility and a deep understanding of multidisciplinary working methods.